Connected  Mathematics™

Ratio, Proportion, and Percent

Student Edition

Glenda Lappan
James T. Fey
William M. Fitzgerald
Susan N. Friel
Elizabeth Difanis Phillips

Developed at Michigan State University

DALE SEYMOUR PUBLICATIONS®
WHITE PLAINS, NEW YORK

Connected Mathematics™ was developed at Michigan State University with the support of National Science Foundation Grant No. MDR 9150217.

This project was supported, in part,
by the
National Science Foundation
Opinions expressed are those of the authors
and not necessarily those of the Foundation

The Michigan State University authors and administration have agreed that all MSU royalties arising from this publication will be devoted to purposes supported by the Department of Mathematics and the MSU Mathematics Education Enrichment Fund.

This book is published by Dale Seymour Publications®, an imprint of Addison Wesley Longman, Inc.

> Dale Seymour Publications
> 10 Bank Street
> White Plains, NY. 10602
> Customer Service: 800 872-1100

Managing Editor: Catherine Anderson
Project Editor: Stacey Miceli
Revision Editor: James P. McAuliffe
Production/Manufacturing Director: Janet Yearian
Production/Manufacturing Coordinators: Claire Flaherty, Alan Noyes
Design Manager: John F. Kelly
Photo Editor: Roberta Spieckerman
Design: PCI, San Antonio, TX
Composition: London Road Design, Palo Alto, CA
Electronic Prepress Revision: A. W. Kingston Publishing Services, Chandler, AZ
Illustrations: Pauline Phung, Margaret Copeland, Ray Godfrey
Cover: Ray Godfrey

Photo Acknowledgements: 8 © Renee Lynn/Photo Researchers, Inc.; 17 © Peter Menzel/Stock, Boston; 18 © Peter Wandermark/Stock, Boston; 32 © Ralph Cowan/Tony Stone Images; 42 © Mitch Wojnarowicz/The Image Works; 45 © R. M. Collins, III/The Image Works; 50 © Erika Stone/Photo Researchers, Inc.; 52 © Lee Snider/The Image Works; 54 © Dion Ogust/The Image Works; 58 © John Coletti/Stock, Boston; 60 © Alvin Staffan/National Audubon Society/Photo Researchers, Inc.; 65 © Peter Menzel/Stock, Boston; 79 © Don Rypka/UPI/Bettmann Newsphoto

DALE SEYMOUR PUBLICATIONS®

Order number 45830
ISBN 1-57232-635-2

4 5 6 7 8 9 10-BA-01 00 99

The Connected Mathematics Project Staff

Project Directors

James T. Fey
University of Maryland

William M. Fitzgerald
Michigan State University

Susan N. Friel
University of North Carolina at Chapel Hill

Glenda Lappan
Michigan State University

Elizabeth Difanis Phillips
Michigan State University

Project Manager

Kathy Burgis
Michigan State University

Technical Coordinator

Judith Martus Miller
Michigan State University

Curriculum Development Consultants

David Ben-Chaim
Weizmann Institute

Alex Friedlander
Weizmann Institute

Eleanor Geiger
University of Maryland

Jane Mitchell
University of North Carolina at Chapel Hill

Anthony D. Rickard
Alma College

Collaborating Teachers/Writers

Mary K. Bouck
Portland, Michigan

Jacqueline Stewart
Okemos, Michigan

Graduate Assistants

Scott J. Baldridge
Michigan State University

Angie S. Eshelman
Michigan State University

M. Faaiz Gierdien
Michigan State University

Jane M. Keiser
Indiana University

Angela S. Krebs
Michigan State University

James M. Larson
Michigan State University

Ronald Preston
Indiana University

Tat Ming Sze
Michigan State University

Sarah Theule-Lubienski
Michigan State University

Jeffrey J. Wanko
Michigan State University

Evaluation Team

Mark Hoover
Michigan State University

Diane V. Lambdin
Indiana University

Sandra K. Wilcox
Michigan State University

Judith S. Zawojewski
National-Louis University

Teacher/Assessment Team

Kathy Booth
Waverly, Michigan

Anita Clark
Marshall, Michigan

Julie Faulkner
Traverse City, Michigan

Theodore Gardella
Bloomfield Hills, Michigan

Yvonne Grant
Portland, Michigan

Linda R. Lobue
Vista, California

Suzanne McGrath
Chula Vista, California

Nancy McIntyre
Troy, Michigan

Mary Beth Schmitt
Traverse City, Michigan

Linda Walker
Tallahassee, Florida

Software Developer

Richard Burgis
East Lansing, Michigan

Development Center Directors

Nicholas Branca
San Diego State University

Dianne Briars
Pittsburgh Public Schools

Frances R. Curcio
New York University

Perry Lanier
Michigan State University

J. Michael Shaughnessy
Portland State University

Charles Vonder Embse
Central Michigan University

Special thanks to the students and teachers at these pilot schools!

Baker Demonstration School
Evanston, Illinois

Bertha Vos Elementary School
Traverse City, Michigan

Blair Elementary School
Traverse City, Michigan

Bloomfield Hills Middle School
Bloomfield Hills, Michigan

Brownell Elementary School
Flint, Michigan

Catlin Gabel School
Portland, Oregon

Cherry Knoll Elementary School
Traverse City, Michigan

Cobb Middle School
Tallahassee, Florida

Courtade Elementary School
Traverse City, Michigan

Duke School for Children
Durham, North Carolina

DeVeaux Junior High School
Toledo, Ohio

East Junior High School
Traverse City, Michigan

Eastern Elementary School
Traverse City, Michigan

Eastlake Elementary School
Chula Vista, California

Eastwood Elementary School
Sturgis, Michigan

Elizabeth City Middle School
Elizabeth City, North Carolina

Franklinton Elementary School
Franklinton, North Carolina

Frick International Studies Academy
Pittsburgh, Pennsylvania

Gundry Elementary School
Flint, Michigan

Hawkins Elementary School
Toledo, Ohio

Hilltop Middle School
Chula Vista, California

Holmes Middle School
Flint, Michigan

Interlochen Elementary School
Traverse City, Michigan

Los Altos Elementary School
San Diego, California

Louis Armstrong Middle School
East Elmhurst, New York

McTigue Junior High School
Toledo, Ohio

National City Middle School
National City, California

Norris Elementary School
Traverse City, Michigan

Northeast Middle School
Minneapolis, Minnesota

Oak Park Elementary School
Traverse City, Michigan

Old Mission Elementary School
Traverse City, Michigan

Old Orchard Elementary School
Toledo, Ohio

Portland Middle School
Portland, Michigan

Reizenstein Middle School
Pittsburgh, Pennsylvania

Sabin Elementary School
Traverse City, Michigan

Shepherd Middle School
Shepherd, Michigan

Sturgis Middle School
Sturgis, Michigan

Terrell Lane Middle School
Louisburg, North Carolina

Tierra del Sol Middle School
Lakeside, California

Traverse Heights Elementary School
Traverse City, Michigan

University Preparatory Academy
Seattle, Washington

Washington Middle School
Vista, California

Waverly East Intermediate School
Lansing, Michigan

Waverly Middle School
Lansing, Michigan

West Junior High School
Traverse City, Michigan

Willow Hill Elementary School
Traverse City, Michigan

Contents

Comparing and Scaling

Arvind and Mariah are testing four different orange juice recipes to see which tastes best. Mix A has 2 cups of orange juice concentrate and 3 cups of water; mix B has 1 cup of concentrate and 4 cups of water; mix C has 4 cups of concentrate and 8 cups of water; and mix D has 3 cups of concentrate and 5 cups of water. Which mix will taste the most "orangey"?

Madeline's car went 580 miles with 19 gallons of gas. Luis's car went 452 miles with 15.5 gallons of gas. Which car got better gas mileage?

South Dakota has a population of 721,000 and a land area of 75,896 square miles. North Dakota has a population of 638,000 and a land area of 68,994 square miles. Which of these states is more densely populated?

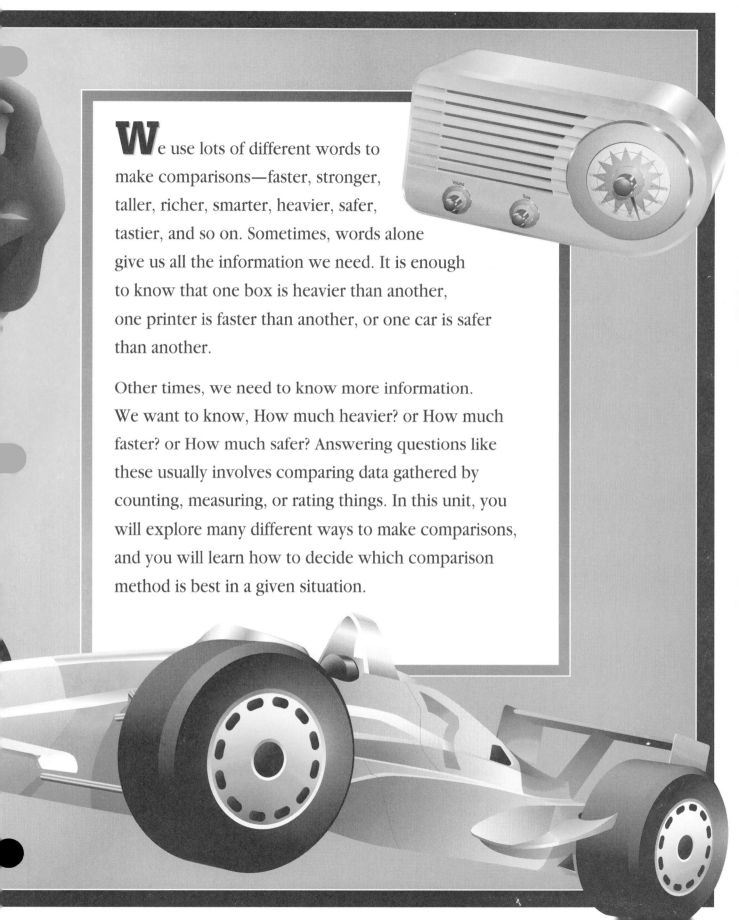

We use lots of different words to make comparisons—faster, stronger, taller, richer, smarter, heavier, safer, tastier, and so on. Sometimes, words alone give us all the information we need. It is enough to know that one box is heavier than another, one printer is faster than another, or one car is safer than another.

Other times, we need to know more information. We want to know, How much heavier? or How much faster? or How much safer? Answering questions like these usually involves comparing data gathered by counting, measuring, or rating things. In this unit, you will explore many different ways to make comparisons, and you will learn how to decide which comparison method is best in a given situation.

Mathematical Highlights

In *Comparing and Scaling,* **you will develop several methods for comparing quantities, and you will use these methods to solve interesting problems.**

● As you look at cola advertisements, you see that there are often several ways to express a comparison.

● By working with survey data, you explore the many ways to express comparisons and practice determining which way is best in a given situation.

● As you examine data from a national survey and compare them with data from your class, you see that percents are useful for comparing populations of different sizes.

● Solving problems about preparing meals at a school camp gives you practice scaling ratios up and down.

● Your knowledge of ratios allows you to simulate a method biologists use to estimate animal populations.

● Using a special type of comparison called a *rate,* you solve problems involving fuel economy, bicycle speed, and bead prices.

● What you know about ratios, rates, and percents helps you compare a human to a *Tyrannosaurus rex* and use rules of thumb to solve problems.

● Solving *proportions* helps you develop a plan for choosing delegates to a national environmental conference.

Using a Calculator

In this unit, you will be able to use your calculator to find scale factors between similar figures, find coordinates of expanded figures and scale models, and measure inaccessible lengths. As you work in Connected Mathematics you can decide when a calculator would be helpful in solving a problem.

Making Comparisons

It's easy to decide which of two numbers is larger or smaller. However, it's not as easy to decide on the best way to explain *how much* larger or smaller one number is than another—especially when one or both of the numbers are fractions. In this unit, you will learn several ways to compare numbers.

1.1 Writing Ads

In their advertisements, companies often refer to surveys to show that people prefer their product over a competitor's product. An ad for Bolda Cola starts like this:

To complete the ad, Bolda Cola wants to report the results of their taste tests. A copywriter from the advertising department has proposed four possible concluding statements.

In taste tests, people who preferred **BOLDA COLA** outnumbered those who preferred **Cola Nola** by a ratio of **3** to **2**.

 In taste tests, people who preferred **BOLDA COLA** outnumbered those preferring **Cola Nola** by a ratio of **17,139 to 11,426.**

 In taste tests, **5713** more people preferred **BOLDA COLA** to **Cola Nola**.

In taste tests, **60%** prefer  **BOLDA COLA** to **Cola Nola**.

Problem 1.1

A. Describe what you think each of the four statements means. Explain how each shows a comparison. Be sure to tell *what* is being compared and *how* it is being compared.

B. Is it possible that all four advertising claims are based on the same survey data? Explain your answer.

C. Which comparison do you think is the most accurate way to report the survey data? Why?

D. Which comparison do you think would be the most effective advertisement for Bolda Cola? Why?

■ **Problem 1.1 Follow-Up**

Write two more statements comparing the popularity of the two colas. Explain each statement you write.

1.2 Targeting an Audience

Many middle and high school students work delivering papers, mowing lawns, or baby-sitting. Students who have money of their own to spend are a common target audience for radio and television ads. Information about the amount of time students spend watching television or listening to the radio influences how companies who want to sell products to them spend their advertising dollars. Advertisers want to know which type of media will best get their message across.

Be the first kid on your block to own an ACME SKATEBOARD. They're cool!

Problem 1.2

A survey of 100 students at Neilson Middle School found that 60 students prefer watching television in the evening and 40 prefer listening to the radio.

A. Read the statements below about how Neilson students prefer to spend their evenings. Tell whether each statement accurately reports the results of the survey. Explain your answers.

1. 6 out of 10 students prefer television to radio.

2. Students prefer radio to television by a ratio of 4 to 6.

3. Students who prefer television outnumber those who prefer radio by 20.

4. Students who prefer television outnumber those who prefer radio by a ratio of 3 to 2.

5. The number of students who prefer watching television is 1.5 times the number who prefer listening to radio.

6. 40% of the students prefer radio to television.

7. $\frac{3}{5}$ of the students prefer television to radio.

B. If you were writing a paper to convince local merchants that they would reach more students by advertising on the radio than on television, which statement from above would you use? Why?

C. Imagine that you are the advertising director for a television station in the town where Neilson is located. You have been asked to prepare a report for a meeting between your ad department and a large local skateboard manufacturer. Which accurate statement from above would you use to try to convince the manufacturer to advertise on your station? Why?

Conduct a quick survey in your class to find out how many students prefer watching television in the evening and how many prefer listening to the radio. Record the results in a table.

1. For each statement in part A on page 7, write a similar statement about your class data.

2. In what ways is your class data similar to the Neilson data? In what ways is your data different?

3. You may have heard people talk about an interest group *manipulating* data to promote their cause. This doesn't mean they used incorrect data, but that they made careful decisions about which data to use and how to represent the data to support their cause. How could you manipulate your class data to persuade local merchants to advertise on radio rather than on television?

1.3 Getting the Message Across

Camping is a popular activity in the United States. Every year, millions of families visit national, state, and local parks to enjoy the wonders of nature. While some of these visitors "rough it" in tents, many prefer cabins, trailers, and campers—bringing a few comforts of home to the wilderness.

The following table gives data on the popularity of camping for several age groups in the United States. It shows the number of people in each age group who go camping at least twice a year. The numbers in the table are projections based on data from a sample of 10,000 households.

Camping Data

	Ages 12–17	Ages 18–24	Ages 25–34
Total in the age group	21,304,000	26,650,000	41,808,000
Number who camp at least twice a year	5,336,000	4,767,000	10,000,000

Source: National Sporting Goods Association, as found in the *Statistical Abstract of the United States 1995*. Published by the Bureau of the Census, Washington, D.C., p. 260.

Problem 1.3

Suppose you were asked to write a news story about the popularity of camping in the United States based on the data in the table.

A. What headline would you use for your story? What would your first sentence be?

B. Write five statements you could use in your story to compare the popularity of camping among people in the three age groups. In each statement, be clear about which groups you are comparing. Your comparisons should be specific and based on mathematics.

■ Problem 1.3 Follow-Up

According to the data, what percent of people from age 12 to 34 go camping at least twice a year?

As you work on these ACE questions, use your calculator whenever you need it.

Applications

In 1–4, use the following information: Oksana surveyed her class to find out how students spend their time over a weekend. On Friday, she distributed a list of activities and asked her classmates to keep track of how many hours they spent from midnight on Friday to midnight on Sunday doing each activity. On Monday, she collected the data and found the mean number of hours the students spent in each category. She put her results in a table.

Weekend Activities

Activity	Average number of hours
Sleeping	18.4 hours
Eating	3.5 hours
Recreation	7.4 hours
Talking on the phone	0.6 hours
Watching television	3.7 hours
Doing chores or homework	4.7 hours
Other	9.7 hours

In 1–3, use Oksana's data to fill in the blanks to create an accurate statement.

1. In comparing time spent watching television to recreation time, students spent more time ——————— than ——————— by a ratio of ——————— to ———————.

2. The number of hours spent watching television is about ——————— times the number of hours spent doing chores or homework.

3. In comparing time spent eating and sleeping to time spent in recreation and watching television, ——————— percent of the weekend was spent ———————, and ——————— percent was spent ———————.

4. Make up a comparison like those in questions 1–3 about the data in Oksana's table. Tell why you think your comparison is interesting.

Connections

5. Below is a drawing of the spinner used in the Big Wheel game at the Waverly Middle School fun night. The chart shows the data from 236 spins of the Big Wheel.

Spin Results

Win	Lose
46	190

a. Use the data in the table to make a ratio comparison, a percent comparison, and a difference comparison.

b. Choose one of the methods of comparison from part a (ratios, percents, or differences). Think of a situation in which this method would be an effective way to report the spin results. Explain your reasoning.

c. Explain how you could find the probability of getting a win in one spin of the spinner without using the data in the chart.

d. Do the results in the table seem to agree with or contradict the probability statement you made in part c?

6. Copy the number line below. Add labels for 0.25, $\frac{6}{8}$, $1\frac{3}{4}$, and 1.3.

7. Write two fractions with different denominators so that one fraction is less than the other. Tell which fraction is larger.

8. Write a fraction and a decimal so that the fraction is greater than the decimal.

In 9–11, rewrite the pair of numbers, inserting < or > to make a true statement.

9. $\frac{4}{5}$ $\frac{11}{12}$ **10.** 2.5 0.259   **11.** $1\frac{3}{4}$ 1.5

Extensions

12. The first row of the table below shows the number of hours visitors spent in federal recreation areas in 1980 and 1990. Some of these federal recreation areas are managed by the National Forest Service. The second row of the table shows how many of the hours from the first row were spent in National Forest Service areas.

Hours Spent in Recreation Areas

	Visitor hours in 1980	Visitor hours in 1990
Federal recreation areas	6,367,000,000	7,567,000,000
National Forest Service areas	2,819,000,000	3,157,000,000

Source: 1980, the U.S. Heritage Conservation and Recreation Service; 1990, the U.S. National Park Service; as found in the *Statistical Abstract of the United States 1995.* Published by the Bureau of the Census, Washington, D.C., p. 251.

a. Write statements for each year, 1980 and 1990, comparing visitor hours in National Forest Service areas to visitor hours in all federal recreation areas.

b. Do the statements you wrote show visitor hours in National Forest Service areas growing or declining in comparison to visitor hours in federal recreation areas? Explain how you got your answer.

13. The table below shows the number of new books and new editions published in several subject areas in 1980 and 1990.

New Books and New Editions

Subject	Published in 1980	Published in 1990
Art	1691	1262
Education	1011	1039
Fiction	2835	5764
Juvenile	2859	5172
Literature	1686	2049
Total new books and new editions	**42,377**	**46,738**

Source: *Publishers Weekly,* as found in the *Statistical Abstract of the United States 1995.* Published by the Bureau of the Census, Washington, D.C., p. 580.

a. Compare the change in the number of new books and new editions published in 1980 and 1990 in each subject area by computing differences.

b. For 1980, find the percent of all new books and new editions that were published in each subject area.

c. For 1990, find the percent of all new books and new editions that were published in each subject area.

d. Describe how the percent of books published in each subject area changed from 1980 to 1990.

e. Which method of comparison (differences or percents) would you choose if you were a librarian making a case for an increased budget for fiction books in your library? Explain your reasoning.

f. Which method of comparison would you choose if you were a reporter writing an article about trends in the book-publishing business over time? Explain your reasoning.

14. Write an advertisement that will be more effective than the one below.

Three thousand seven hundred fourteen out of four thousand nine hundred fifty-two dentists surveyed recommend sugarless gum to their patients who chew gum.

Sugarless Gum

Mathematical Reflections

In this investigation, you explored several ways of comparing numbers. Here are five methods for making comparisons, with examples:

Ratios: In taste tests, people who preferred Bolda Cola outnumbered those who preferred Cola Nola by a ratio of 3 to 2.

Differences: Students who prefer television outnumber those who prefer radio by 20.

Fractions: $\frac{3}{5}$ of cola drinkers prefer Bolda Cola to Cola Nola.

Percents: 28% of people aged 12–17 go camping.

Scaling: The number of students who prefer watching television is 1.5 times the number who prefer listening to the radio.

These questions will help you summarize what you have learned:

1 Give another example of each type of comparison listed above.

2 What information do you get from a ratio comparison that you don't get from a difference comparison?

Think about your answers to these questions, discuss your ideas with other students and your teacher, and then write a summary of your findings in your journal.

Comparing by Finding Percents

What do you like to do during your free time? Do you enjoy exercising or playing sports? A 1991 survey found that the five most popular sports activities in the United States are bicycle riding, camping, exercise walking, fishing, and swimming.

Think about this!

With your class, discuss the kinds of sports activities you like to participate in. Identify four or five activities that are different from those mentioned in the national survey. List these activities, along with the activities found in the national survey, on the board. Then, survey the class, asking each student which activities he or she participates in more than once a year. Tally the results for boys and girls separately. Save the data so that you can compare your class with the national survey in a later problem.

The problems in this investigation ask you to make comparisons about data. In particular, you are asked to think about ways to use percents to make comparisons.

Remember that percent means "out of 100." You can find a percent by first dividing to find a decimal. For example, the table below shows the number of males in the United States and the number of them who swim. To find the percent of males who swim, first divide the number of male swimmers by the total number of males to get a decimal. Then, round the decimal to the nearest hundredth and change the decimal to a percent.

Males in the U.S.	111,851,000
Males who swim	27,713,000

For this data, $27,713,000 \div 111,851,000 = 0.24776711$, which rounded to the nearest hundredth is 0.25. The decimal 0.25 is equivalent to 25%, so about 25% of males swim.

2.1 Comparing Leisure Activities

The table below gives data about participation in the five most popular sports activities in the United States—bicycle riding, camping, exercise walking, fishing, and swimming. The numbers are projections based on a 1993 survey of 10,000 households. The survey counted anyone 7 years old or older who participated in an activity more than once per year. Some people participated in more than one activity. The numbers in the "Total in group" row are the total number of people in the United States population in each group.

Participation in Sports Activities

Activity	Males	Females	Ages 12–17	Ages 55–64
Bicycle riding	24,562,000	23,357,000	8,794,000	2,030,000
Camping	23,165,000	19,533,000	5,336,000	2,355,000
Exercise walking	21,054,000	43,373,000	2,816,000	7,782,000
Fishing	30,449,000	14,885,000	4,945,000	3,156,000
Swimming	27,713,000	33,640,000	10,874,000	2,756,000
Total in group	**111,851,000**	**118,555,000**	**21,304,000**	**20,922,000**

Source: National Sporting Goods Association, as found in the *Statistical Abstract of the United States 1995*. Published by the Bureau of the Census, Washington, D.C., p. 260.

Problem 2.1

In the table above, look for interesting patterns in the data for males and females and in the data for the two age groups.

A. Why don't the numbers in the columns add to the given totals?

B. Write three statements that use percents to make comparisons about the numbers of male and female participants in the various activities. Explain how you found the percents.

C. Write three statements that use percents to make comparisons about the numbers of teenage and older-adult participants in the various activities.

D. Write three statements that make comparisons about the data without using percents.

1. Explain how you might decide when percents would be a good way to make a comparison and when other forms of comparison would be better. Use examples if they help explain your ideas.

2. Can you compare the participation of teenage boys in these activities to the participation of older-adult women by using the data in the table? Explain.

2.2 Comparing Your Class to the Nation

Statistics that are based on data from a small group of people, or from people who live in a particular area, may be quite different from statistics based on a national survey. For example, if there is a lake or another body of water in your area, fishing may be more popular in your class than in the nation as a whole.

In this problem, you will compare your class data with the data from the national survey. When the total numbers in two data sets are very different, representing the data values as percents of a total is a useful way to compare the data sets. Finding percents is a way of creating a common scale for two data sets by expressing all the data values as numbers "out of 100."

Did you know?

Here are some interesting percents:

- About 71% of the earth is covered by water.
- Females make up about 51.3% of the population of the United States.
- About 99% of all homes in the United States have at least one TV set, about 66% have at least two TV sets, and 65% get cable television.
- Of all the computers in the world, about 43% are in use in the United States, 22% in Europe, and 7% in Japan.
- More than 70% of the waste produced in the United States ends up in landfills.

Source: *1996 Information Please Almanac.* Ed. Otto Johnson. New York: Houghton Mifflin, 1995.

Problem 2.2

You conducted a class survey at the beginning of this investigation. Now, organize the results for bicycle riding, camping, exercise walking, fishing, and swimming into a table similar to the one on page 17. Your table should have separate columns for males and females.

A. Look back at the three statements you wrote in part B of Problem 2.1 comparing the numbers of male and female participants in the various activities. Now, make the same comparisons for boys and girls in your class.

B. Compare the statements about your class data to the statements about the national data.

C. Write three statements comparing sports activities of all students in your class to those of

   1. 12 to 17 year olds in the national survey

   2. 55 to 64 year olds in the national survey

Problem 2.2 Follow-Up

1. Write a paragraph telling how your class data is like the national data and how it is different. For any ways in which your class data appears to be different from the national data, give reasons why you think your class is different.

2. In your class survey, you added several activities to the five listed in the national survey. Write at least three statements comparing the numbers of boys and girls in your class who participate in these activities.

As you work on these ACE questions, use your calculator whenever you need it.

Applications

In 1–8, use the following information: A homeroom class of 32 eighth graders at Springbrook Middle School completed a survey about their participation in team sports. Each student was asked to list any sport he or she liked to play. The results for four of the most popular sports are given in this table.

Participation in Team Sports

Sport	Female	Male
Basketball	14	13
Track and field	7	13
Softball	10	8
Football	4	11
Total surveyed	**17**	**15**

1. What fraction of the class is female?

2. What percent of the class is female?

3. What percent of the class is male?

4. Write two statements comparing participation in basketball to participation in football.

5. In which sport does the greatest percent of the class participate?

6. In which sport does the greatest percent of the male students participate? Explain your answer.

7. In which sports is there a greater percent of female participation than male participation? Explain your answer.

8. If the percents of participation in these sports for all students at Springbrook are approximately the same as the percents for this class, about how many of the 368 female students in the school like to play softball?

In 9–15, use the table below, which shows the national data on exercise walking.

Participation in Exercise Walking

Activity	Males	Females	Ages 12–17	Ages 55–64
Exercise walking	21,054,000	43,373,000	2,816,000	7,782,000
Total in group	**111,851,000**	**118,555,000**	**21,304,000**	**20,922,000**

Source: National Sporting Goods Association, as found in the *Statistical Abstract of the United States 1995.*
Published by the Bureau of the Census, Washington, D.C., p. 260.

9. What percent of the 55–64 age group walks for exercise?

10. What percent of the 12–17 age group walks for exercise?

11. What percent of males walks for exercise?

12. Write a statement comparing the number of males who walk for exercise to the number of females who walk for exercise.

13. Write a statement comparing the number of 12 to 17 year olds who walk for exercise to the number of 55 to 64 year olds who walk for exercise.

14. Look back at your class data. Describe how your class data on exercise walking is similar to the national data and how it is different.

15. Suppose your class data reflected the same percents as the national data. How many males and females in your class would exercise walk?

Connections

16. Below are floor plans for two college dorm rooms. One is for two students, and the other is for one student.

    a. Are the floors of the two rooms similar rectangles? Explain.

    b. For each room, what is the floor area?

    c. Which room gives each student the most space?

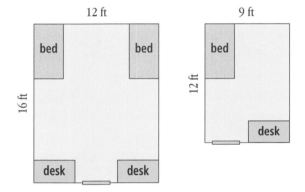

17. **a.** Plot the points (8, 6), (8, 22), and (24, 14) on grid paper. Connect them to form a triangle.

    b. Draw the triangle you get when you apply the rule (0.5*x*, 0.5*y*) to the three points from part a.

    c. How are the triangles from parts a and b related?

    d. The area of the smaller triangle is what percent of the area of the larger triangle?

    e. The area of the larger triangle is what percent of the area of the smaller triangle?

18. In a–f, rewrite the sentence, replacing the question mark with a number that makes the sentence true.

   a. $\frac{3}{4} < \frac{?}{12}$

   b. $\frac{3}{4} = \frac{?}{12}$

   c. $\frac{3}{4} > \frac{?}{12}$

   d. $\frac{5}{9} < \frac{?}{15}$

   e. $\frac{5}{9} = \frac{?}{15}$

   f. $\frac{5}{9} > \frac{?}{15}$

   g. Explain your strategies for solving these problems.

19. Write two fractions with different denominators and a sum of $\frac{4}{5}$.

20. Write two decimal numbers with three or fewer digits each and a sum of 12.36.

21. Write a decimal number and a fraction with a sum of 0.593.

22. A store is having a 30% off sale. How would you determine an item's sale price?

Extensions

In 23 and 24, look at the table of data about participation in sports activities on page 17.

23. Which sports activity has the greatest percent of participation by females? Which has the greatest percent of participation by males?

24. Which sports activity is most popular among the 12–17 age group? Explain.

25. Kent's department store is having a Super Saturday Sale during which every item is 25% off. When you walk in the door, a salesperson hands you a coupon for an additional 10% off the reduced price of any item. Your friend says, "Wow—if you buy something with your coupon, you will get 35% off the original price!" Is your friend correct? Why or why not?

26. At Kent's department store (from question 25), you decide to buy a T-shirt with an original price of $20. The sales clerk first uses your coupon to reduce the original price by 10% and then applies the 25% discount. Did you save more than you would have if the clerk had applied the 25% discount first and then used the 10% off coupon? Explain your answer.

Mathematical Reflections

In this investigation, you used percents to make comparisons. You compared data for males and females and for teenagers and older adults. You developed your skill in making comparisons and in deciding what kinds of comparisons make sense. These questions will help you summarize what you have learned:

1 Give an example of a situation in which it makes sense to use percents to make comparisons.

2 Using your example from part 1, show how to make a comparison using percents.

3 Explain why percents are useful for making comparisons.

4 Give an example of a situation in which you think another form of comparison is better than percents. Explain your reasoning.

5 Can you find a percent comparison from a ratio comparison? Explain how, or tell what additional information you would need.

Think about your answers to these questions, discuss your ideas with other students and your teacher, and then write a summary of your findings in your journal.

Comparing by Using Ratios

Another useful way to compare numbers is to form *ratios*. You looked at ratios informally in Investigation 1. In this investigation, you will learn to form and interpret ratios in order to make comparisons. Let's look at some examples of statements containing ratios.

In taste tests, people who preferred Bolda Cola outnumbered those who preferred Cola Nola by a ratio of 3 to 2.

The ratio of boys to girls in our class is 12 boys to 15 girls.

The ratio of boys to students in our class is 12 boys to 27 students.

The ratio of kittens to cats in our neighborhood is $\frac{1}{4}$.

The sign in the hotel lobby says 1 dollar Canadian: 0.85 dollars U.S.

A paint mixture calls for 5 parts blue paint to 2 parts yellow paint.

In these examples, ratios are written in three different ways: using the word "to," as in 5 to 8, using the ":" symbol, as in 5:8, and using fraction notation, as in $\frac{5}{8}$. All three forms—5 to 8, 5:8, and $\frac{5}{8}$—mean that for every five of the first item, there are eight of the second item.

Many real-world problems involve scaling a ratio up or down to find an *equivalent ratio*. This requires finding larger or smaller numbers with the same relationship as the numbers in the original ratio. For example, the ratios 2:3, 4:6, and 6:9 are all equivalent. Suppose a shade of purple paint is made using 2 parts red paint to 3 parts blue. You would get the same shade of purple whether you mixed 2 gallons of red paint to 3 gallons of blue paint, 4 gallons of red paint to 6 gallons of blue paint, or 6 gallons of red paint to 9 gallons of blue paint.

3.1 Mixing Juice

Every year, the seventh grade students at Langston Hughes School go on an outdoor-education camping trip. During the week-long trip, the students study nature and participate in recreational activities. Everyone pitches in to help with the cooking and cleanup.

Arvind and Mariah are in charge of making orange juice for all the campers. They make the juice by mixing water and orange juice concentrate. To find the mix that tastes best, Arvind and Mariah decided to test some recipes on a few of their friends.

Problem 3.1

Arvind and Mariah tested four juice mixes.

Mix A
2 cups concentrate
3 cups cold water

Mix B
1 cup concentrate
4 cups cold water

Mix C
4 cups concentrate
8 cups cold water

Mix D
3 cups concentrate
5 cups cold water

A. Which recipe will make juice that is the most "orangey"? Explain your answer.

B. Which recipe will make juice that is the least "orangey"? Explain your answer.

C. Assume that each camper will get $\frac{1}{2}$ cup of juice. For each recipe, how much concentrate and how much water are needed to make juice for 240 campers? Explain your anwer.

■ Problem 3.1 Follow-Up

1. How did you use ratios in solving Problem 3.1?

2. For each recipe, how much concentrate and how much water is needed to make 1 cup of juice?

Did you know?

Here are some interesting ratios:

- There are about 21 white vans on the road for every purple van.
- In 1994, about 493 music CDs were sold for every 10 albums sold.
- For the first 60 miles of depth, the temperature of the earth increases 1°F for every 100–200 feet.
- The ratio of people 5 to 17 years old in the United States to people 85 years of age or older is about 15 to 1.
- Cigarette smoking accounts for 3 out of 10 deaths due to cancer.

Source: *World Almanac and Book of Facts 1996.* Ed. Robert Famighetti. Mahwa, New Jersey: Funk and Wagnalls, 1995.

3.2 Helping the Cook

The camp cook must buy enough ingredients for all the meals he intends to prepare during the week. One of the cook's most popular meals is spaghetti. The spaghetti recipe he uses calls for canned tomatoes. The CannedStuff store has large cans of tomatoes on sale, five cans for $4.00. The cook says he can make sauce for five to six campers from each can of tomatoes.

Problem 3.2

Suppose you are assigned to help the cook order supplies.

A. How many cans of tomatoes would you advise the cook to buy to make spaghetti for the 240 campers? Explain your answer.

B. How much would these cans of tomatoes cost altogether?

■ Problem 3.2 Follow-Up

1. At the EatMore grocery store, you can buy seven cans of tomatoes for $6.00. The cans are the same size as the cans at CannedStuff. Are the tomatoes at EatMore a better buy than the tomatoes at CannedStuff? Explain your answer.

2. Gus was trying to figure out how to think about the EatMore price of seven cans of tomatoes for $6.00. He divided 7 by 6 and got 1.16666667. He then divided 6 by 7 and got 0.85714286. What does each of these numbers mean in the context of seven cans of tomatoes for $6.00?

3.3 Sharing Pizza

On the last day of camp, the cook served pizza. The camp dining room has two kinds of tables. A large table seats 10 people, and a small table seats 8 people. The cook tells the students who are serving dinner to put four pizzas on each large table and three pizzas on each small table.

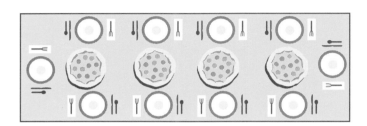
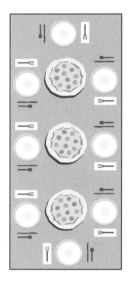

Problem 3.3

A. If the pizzas at a table are shared equally by everyone at the table, will a person sitting at a small table get the same amount of pizza as a person sitting at a large table? Explain your reasoning.

B. The ratio of large tables to small tables in the dining room is 8 to 5. There are exactly enough seats for the 240 campers. How many tables of each kind are there?

■ Problem 3.3 Follow-Up

1. How were ratios helpful in thinking about the problem?

2. How many pizzas will the cook need in order to put four on each large table and three on each small table?

As you work on these ACE questions, use your calculator whenever you need it.

Applications

1. At camp, Miriam learned how to use a pottery wheel. She can make 3 bowls in 2 hours. How long will it take her to make a set of 12 bowls?

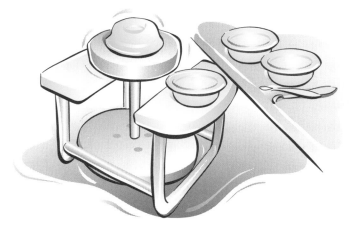

2. The camp cook's favorite recipe for salad dressing calls for 2 tablespoons of lemon juice and 6 tablespoons of olive oil. If the cook wants to make a large batch of salad dressing using 3 cups of oil, how much lemon juice will he need? (There are 16 tablespoons in 1 cup.)

3. You need to buy several dozen avocados to make guacamole dip for a party. At the co-op, you can buy 7 avocados for $6.00. At the Cheapy Food Mart, 5 avocados cost $4.50. At which store will you get the better buy?

4. Friendly Food Store has Cocoa Blast cereal on sale this week at a price of $8.25 for five boxes. Best Food Store is offering the same size box of Cocoa Blast at a price of $3.50 for two boxes. Which offer gives you the most cereal for your money?

5. In the ads for Bolda Cola from Investigation 1, one possible concluding statement says "by a ratio of 3 to 2" and another says "by a ratio of 17,139 to 11,426." These ratios are equivalent. Write four other statements containing ratios equivalent to these ratios.

6. At Louis Armstrong School, Ms. Turini's homeroom has 18 boys and 12 girls.

    a. What is the ratio of boys to girls in Ms. Turini's homeroom?

    b. What is the ratio of girls to boys?

    c. What is the ratio of boys to students in the class?

    d. What is the ratio of students in the class to boys?

7. Lakisha is attending a party at her favorite pizza parlor. Three tables are set up for the guests. After the pizzas are placed on the tables, the guests are asked to sit anywhere they choose. The small table has 5 seats and 2 pizzas, the medium table has 7 seats and 3 pizzas, and the large table has 12 seats and 5 pizzas. The pizzas at each table will be shared equally. Where should Lakisha sit if she is very hungry?

8. Elena works in the animal nursery at the county zoo. The baby monkeys eat a mixture of high-fiber nuggets and high-protein formula. Last month, Elena mixed 4 cups of nuggets and 6 cups of high-protein formula to make the food for each feeding. This month, the monkeys can eat more at each feeding.

    a. If Elena uses 8 cups of nuggets in the new mix, how much high-protein formula should she use?

    b. If Elena uses only 6 cups of nuggets, how much formula should she use?

    c. If Elena uses 7.5 cups of formula, how many cups of nuggets should she use?

In 9–11, use the apple juice recipes below.

Mix W
3 cups concentrate
4 cups cold water

Mix X
3 cup concentrate
5 cups cold water

Mix Y
6 cups concentrate
9 cups cold water

Mix Z
5 cups concentrate
8 cups cold water

9. a. If you made a single batch of mix W, what fraction of the batch would be concentrate? Answer the same question for mixes X, Y, and Z.

b. Rewrite your answers to part a as percents.

10. Which recipe would make the most "appley" juice?

11. If you made only 1 cup of mix W, how much water and how much concentrate would you need? Answer the same question for mixes X, Y, and Z.

Connections

12. The diagram below illustrates the equivalence of two fractions. Find the missing numerator.

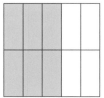 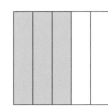

$$\frac{?}{10} = \frac{3}{5}$$

In 13–18, replace the question mark with a number to make a true statement.

13. $\frac{3}{15} = \frac{?}{30}$

14. $\frac{1}{2} = \frac{?}{20}$

15. $\frac{?}{20} = \frac{3}{5}$

16. $\frac{18}{30} = \frac{?}{15}$

17. $\frac{?}{15} = \frac{3}{5}$

18. $\frac{9}{15} = \frac{12}{?}$

19. Illustrate your answer to question 13 by drawing a picture like the one in question 12.

In 20–23, replace the question marks with numbers to make a true statement.

20. $\frac{6}{14} = \frac{?}{21} = \frac{?}{28}$

21. $\frac{?}{27} = \frac{8}{36} = \frac{?}{45}$

22. $\frac{?}{20} = \frac{?}{25} = \frac{6}{30}$

23. $\frac{?}{8} = \frac{15}{?} = \frac{24}{32}$

Extensions

24. Here is a drawing of Mr. Stickman.

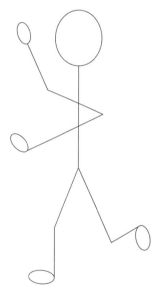

a. Draw a picture of Twiggy Stickman. She is $\frac{1}{2}$ as tall as Mr. Stickman.

b. Draw a picture of Branchy Stickman. He is $\frac{2}{3}$ as tall as Twiggy.

c. Branchy's height is what fraction of Mr. Stickman's height? Explain your reasoning.

d. Use some other form of comparison to rewrite the fraction comparisons in parts a, b, and c.

25. a. What fraction of this square is shaded?

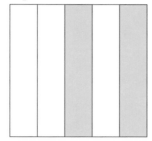

b. What fraction of this square is shaded?

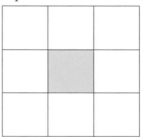

c. Draw a picture to show a fraction with a denominator of 10 that is equivalent to the fraction shaded in part a. Tell what fraction of your drawing is shaded.

d. Draw a picture to show a fraction with a denominator of 27 that is equivalent to the fraction shaded in part b. Tell what fraction of your drawing is shaded.

e. What percent of the square in part a is shaded?

f. What percent of the square in part b is shaded?

g. What is the ratio of the shaded area to the unshaded area in part a?

h. What is the ratio of the shaded area to the unshaded area in part b?

i. The squares in parts a and b are the same size. What is the ratio of the shaded part of the square in part a to the shaded part of the square in part b? Be careful—the answer is not 2 to 1.

Mathematical Reflections

In this investigation, you learned about ratios and about using ratios to make comparisons. These questions will help you summarize what you have learned:

1 Explain how to form a ratio and how ratios can be used to compare two numbers. Use examples to help explain your thinking.

2 What strategy can you use to compare two ratios? Be very specific. Your strategy should allow you to tell whether the two ratios are the same or different. Make up a problem that can be solved by using your strategy.

In Investigation 2, you used percents to make comparisons. In Investigation 3, you used ratios to make comparisons.

3 The percent of orange concentrate in a juice mix is 60%. What is the ratio of concentrate to water in the mix?

4 The ratio of concentrate to water in a juice mix is 3 to 5. What percent of the mix is concentrate?

Think about your answers to these questions, discuss your ideas with other students and your teacher, and then write a summary of your findings in your journal.

Comparing by Finding Rates

In this unit, you have been using percents and ratios to make comparisons. Now, look at these examples of a special kind of comparison you probably encounter frequently:

My mom's new car gets 45 miles per gallon on the expressway.

We need two sandwiches for each person at the picnic.

I earn $3.50 per hour baby-sitting for my neighbor.

Tomatoes are on sale five for $4.00.

The sign above the mystery meat in the cafeteria says 355 calories : 6 ounces.

James can run at a rate of 8.5 kilometers per hour.

Each statement above compares two *different* things: miles to gallons, sandwiches to people, dollars to hours, tomatoes to dollars, calories to ounces, and kilometers to hours. Comparisons of two different things, like those in the statements above, are called **rates.** They tell us the *rate* at which something happens.

You can scale a rate up or down to find an equivalent rate. For example, consider this problem:

Ms. Balog's car gets 45 miles to the gallon on the highway. How much gas will the car use if Ms. Balog drives it 180 miles on the interstate?

Here are two ways you might solve this problem:

Method 1
Divide 180 by 45 to find out how many groups of 45 there are in 180. The result is 4, which means the car will use 4 gallons of gas.

Method 2
Write a ratio and scale up to find the answer:

45 miles per gallon means		45 miles : 1 gallon
or		90 miles : 2 gallons
or		135 miles : 3 gallons
or		180 miles : 4 gallons

The car will use 4 gallons of gas.

4.1 Comparing Fuel Economy

After graduating from the University of Colorado, Luis and Madeline both got teaching jobs in Denver. They each bought a new car for commuting to work, and one afternoon they had a friendly argument about whose car was better. Luis claimed his car was more fuel-efficient. Madeline challenged him to prove his claim. Since they would both be traveling home for Thanksgiving, Luis suggested they use their trips to test the gas mileage of their cars.

Madeline and Luis are from different small towns in southern Colorado, but the routes from Denver to both towns follow I-25 for the first 190 miles to Trinidad.

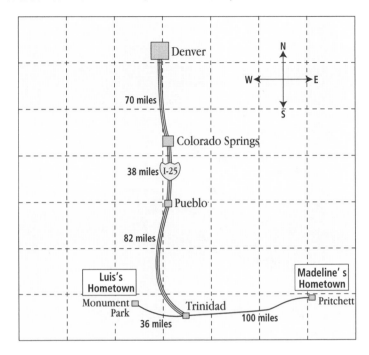

When the two friends returned from the holiday, they compared their fuel economy. Madeline's car used 19 gallons for the trip from Denver to Pritchett and back. Luis's car used only 15.5 gallons of gas for the trip from Denver to Monument Park and back. He said this proved his car was more fuel-efficient than Madeline's. Madeline disagreed.

Problem 4.1

Use the gasoline and mileage data to help settle Madeline and Luis's argument.

Which car do you think is more fuel-efficient on the highway? Explain how you decided and why you think you are correct.

■ Problem 4.1 Follow-Up
Would it make sense to use percents to settle this argument? If so, show how; if not, explain why.

Using Unit Rates

The advertisements below use rates to describe sale prices. How would you compare the value of the offers described in the two ads?

One way to compare rates like these is to do some division to find unit rates. **Unit rates** are rates in which one of the numbers is 1 unit. For example, 55 miles per hour is a unit rate because it tells the number of miles driven for every 1 hour, and 99¢ a pound is a unit rate because it tells the cost for every 1 pound.

Think about this!

Look back at the examples at the beginning of this investigation. Which of these statements are examples of unit rates?

You can compare the advertisements above by finding the *price per CD* (that is, the price for 1 CD) at each store. The price per CD is $5.99 at Music City and $5.71 at CD World.

Problem 4.2

When Madeline and Luis compared the fuel economy of their new cars, they found these rates:

> Madeline's car went 580 miles with 19 gallons of gasoline.
> Luis's car went 452 miles with 15.5 gallons of gasoline.

Use this information to answer the following questions.

A. For each car, find a unit rate describing the mileage. Which car got better gas mileage? In other words, which car went more miles per gallon of gas?

B. Complete a table like the one below, showing the fuel used and the miles covered by each car based on the unit rates you found in part A. We call this kind of table a *rate table*.

Gallons of gas	0	1	2	3	4	5	6	7	8
Miles in Madeline's car									
Miles in Luis's car									

C. Look at the patterns in your table. For each car, write an equation for a rule you can use to predict the miles driven (m) from the gallons of gas used (g).

D. Use the rules you wrote in part C to find the number of miles each car could cover if it used 9.5, 15.5, 19, 23.8, 100, 125, and 150 gallons of gasoline.

■ Problem 4.2 Follow-Up

1. Use your data from B or D to sketch graphs of the (gallons, miles) data for each car.

2. How are your two graphs alike? How are they different?

3. What do you think makes the two graphs different?

4.3 Solving Problems with Rates

Suppose Sascha, a champion bicyclist, wants to see how far he can travel in an hour. He starts timing himself when he reaches a speed of 45 miles per hour. He maintains this speed for 10 minutes. Sascha starts to feel tired and slows down to 30 miles per hour for the next 5 minutes. He then reduces his speed to 25 miles per hour for the next 30 minutes. Finally, Sascha feels exhausted as he finishes the last 15 minutes at 15 miles per hour.

Problem 4.3

A. Make a graph showing Sascha's total distance traveled over time. Use 5-minute time intervals on the *x*-axis.

B. How far did Sascha travel in his 1-hour ride? Explain.

C. If you could maintain a steady speed of 13 miles per hour on a bike, how long would it take you to travel the same distance Sascha traveled in his 1-hour ride?

D. If you were racing Sascha, what constant (steady) speed would you have to maintain to tie him?

■ Problem 4.3 Follow-Up

Can you write a single equation that will allow you to predict Sascha's total distance at any time during his 1-hour ride? Why or why not?

Did you know?

The highest speed ever recorded on a pedal-powered bike was 152.284 miles per hour. John Howard performed this amazing feat on July 20, 1985, at Bonneville Salt Flats, Utah. He was able to reach this speed by following a car, which acted as a windshield for him and his bike.

Source: *Guinness Book of Records 1994*. Ed. Peter Matthews. New York: Bantam Books, 1994, p. 615.

4.4 Buying Beads

Stores often use rates in their advertisements. Rather than using unit rates, advertisements often give the cost for several items. For example, a grocery store might advertise five cans of tomatoes for $4.00. Such advertisements may entice customers to buy more. But, even though an ad gives the price for several items, you can usually buy fewer items at the same rate.

The owner of a crafts store believes that price displays like the one below get her customers' attention. However, when customers want amounts other than 10, 15, or 20 beads, figuring the bill is not easy.

Craft Beads

Spheres: 12¢ for 20
Cubes: 12¢ for 15
Cylinders: 8¢ for 10

Problem 4.4

Write an equation relating the cost (c) and the number of beads (x) for each type of bead:

Spheres: $c =$ _____

Cubes: $c =$ _____

Cylinders: $c =$ _____

■ Problem 4.4 Follow-Up

For each type of bead, you could find two unit rates. You could find the number of beads for each unit of cost (in other words, for each cent), and you could find the cost for each bead.

1. Which unit rate would be most useful if you were trying to figure out the number of beads you could buy with a certain amount of money?

2. Which unit rate would be most useful if you were trying to figure out how much money a certain number of beads costs?

As you work on these ACE questions, use your calculator whenever you need it.

Applications

1. The manager of Quality Dairy stores says it takes 1000 pounds of milk to make 100 pounds of cheddar cheese.

a. Make a rate table showing the amount of milk needed to make 100 pounds to 1000 pounds of cheddar cheese in increments of 100 pounds (this means 100 pounds, 200 pounds, 300 pounds, and so on).

b. Make a graph showing the relationship between pounds of milk and pounds of cheddar cheese. Think carefully about which variable should go on each axis.

c. Find a unit rate relating pounds of milk to pounds of cheddar cheese. Use the rate you find to write an equation relating pounds of milk (m) to pounds of cheese (c).

d. Give one advantage of each form of representation—the graph, the table, and the rule.

2. The Quality Dairy manager said it takes 700 pounds of milk to make 100 pounds of cottage cheese.

a. Make a rate table showing the amount of milk needed to make 100 pounds to 1000 pounds of cottage cheese in increments of 100 pounds.

b. Make a graph showing the relationship between pounds of milk and pounds of cottage cheese. Think carefully about which variable should go on each axis.

c. Find a unit rate relating pounds of milk to pounds of cottage cheese. Use the rate you find to write an equation relating pounds of milk (m) to pounds of cottage cheese (c).

d. Compare the graph in this question to the graph in question 1. Explain how they are alike and how they are different. What is the cause of the differences between the two graphs?

3. The world-champion milk producer in 1993 was a 6-year-old cow from Oxford, New Hampshire. The cow, Tullando Royalty Maxima, produced 58,952 pounds of milk in that year!

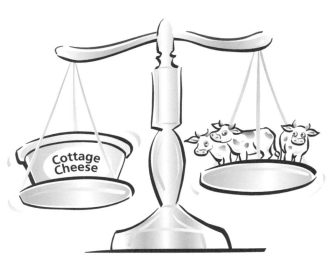

a. Look back at your answers to question 2. How much cottage cheese could be made from the milk that Maxima produced during 1993?

b. The average weight of a dairy cow is 1400 pounds. How many dairy cows would be needed to equal the weight of the cottage cheese made from Maxima's yearly production of milk?

c. One gallon of milk weighs about 8.6 pounds. Suppose a milk bucket holds about 3 gallons. About how many milk buckets would Maxima's *daily* production of milk fill?

d. One pound of milk fills about two glasses. About how many glasses of milk could you fill with Maxima's *daily* production of milk?

4. On their morning commutes to work, Golda travels 10 miles in about 15 minutes and Dale travels 23 miles in about 30 minutes. Who has the faster average speed?

5. Rolanda and Louise rode bikes at a steady pace along a narrow road with no traffic. Rolanda rode 8 miles in 32 minutes. Louise rode 2 miles in 10 minutes. Who was riding the fastest?

6. Fasiz and Kari were driving at the same speed along a bumpy country road. Fasiz drove 8 kilometers in 24 minutes. How far did Kari drive in 6 minutes?

7. Students at Langston Hughes School rode to camp on several buses. On the long dirt road leading to the camp, the buses covered only 6 miles in 10 minutes.

a. At this speed, how long would it take the buses to cover 18 miles?

b. At this speed, how far would the buses go in 15 minutes?

8. a. Mara's car can be driven 580 miles with 20 gallons of gasoline. Make a rate table showing the number of miles her car can be driven with 1, 2, 3, . . . , 10 gallons of gas.

b. Joel's car can be driven 450 miles with 15 gallons of gasoline. Make a rate table showing the number of miles his car can be driven with 1, 2, 3, . . . , 10 gallons of gas.

9. The local grocery store has videotapes on sale, $3.00 for 2 tapes. You have $20.

    a. How many tapes can you buy?

    b. If there is a 7% sales tax on the tapes, how many can you buy?

Connections

10. Franky's Fudge Factory provides customers with the following information about the calories in their fudge.

Caloric Content of Franky's Fudge

Grams of fudge	Calories
50	150
150	450
300	900
500	1500

    a. Fiona ate 75 grams of fudge. How many calories did she consume?

    b. Freddy consumed 1000 calories worth of fudge. How many grams of fudge did he eat?

    c. Describe a rule you can use to find the number of calories in any number of grams of Franky's fudge.

11. This table shows how to convert liters to quarts.

Liters	Quarts
1	1.06
4	4.24
5	5.30
9	9.54

    a. About how many liters are in 5.5 quarts?

    b. About how many quarts are in 5.5 liters?

    c. Write an equation that relates liters (L) and quarts (Q).

In 12–16, find a unit rate, and use it to write an equation relating the two variables.

12. 12 cents for 20 beads   **13.** 8 cents for 10 nails

14. 450 miles on 15 gallons of gasoline

15. 3 cups of water for 2 cups of orange concentrate

16. $4.00 for 5 cans of soup

In 17 and 18, replace the question mark with a number to make a true sentence.

17. $\frac{4}{9} \times ? = 1\frac{1}{3}$ **18.** $? \times 2.25 = 90$

19. Write two fractions whose product is between 10 and 11.

20. Write two decimals whose product is between 1 and 2.

21. The table of data below shows the mean times that students in one seventh grade class spend on several activities during the weekend.

   a. The *stacked bar graph* on the next page was made using the data from the table. Explain how it was constructed.

   b. Suppose you are writing a report summarizing the class's data. You have space for either the table or the graph, but not both. What is one advantage of including the table? What is one advantage of including the stacked bar graph?

How We Spend Our Weekends

Category	Boys	Girls	All students
Sleeping	18.8 hours	18.2 hours	18.4 hours
Eating	4.0 hours	2.7 hours	3.5 hours
Recreation	7.8 hours	6.9 hours	7.4 hours
Talking on the phone	0.5 hours	0.7 hours	0.6 hours
Watching TV	4.2 hours	3.0 hours	3.7 hours
Doing chores, homework	3.6 hours	5.8 hours	4.7 hours
Other	9.1 hours	10.7 hours	9.7 hours

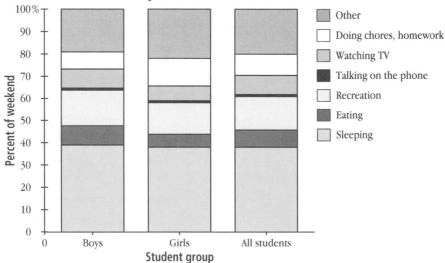

How We Spend Our Weekends

Legend:
- Other
- Doing chores, homework
- Watching TV
- Talking on the phone
- Recreation
- Eating
- Sleeping

Y-axis: Percent of weekend

X-axis: Student group (Boys, Girls, All students)

Extensions

22. A cider mill has pressed a 240-liter vat of apple juice. The mill has many kinds of containers in which to pack juice.

a. The mill owner wants to package the entire vat of juice in containers of the same size. Complete this table to show the number of containers of each size needed to hold the entire vat of juice.

Volume of container (liters)	10	4	2	1	$\frac{1}{2}$	$\frac{1}{4}$	$\frac{1}{10}$
Number of containers needed	24						

b. Write an equation that describes the relationship between the volume of the container (v) and the number of containers needed (n) to hold 240 liters of juice.

23. A chemistry student is analyzing the contents of rust, and she finds that it is made of iron and oxygen. She tests several amounts of rust and produces the following data. (Note: g is the abbreviation for grams.)

Amount of rust (g)	Amount of iron (g)	Amount of oxygen (g)
50	35.0	15.0
100	70.0	30.0
135	94.5	40.5
150	105.0	45.0

a. If the student analyzed 400 grams of rust, how much iron and how much oxygen would she find?

b. Is the ratio of the amount of iron to the amount of rust constant? If so, what is the ratio?

Mathematical Reflections

In this investigation, you learned about a special way to compare quantities called a *rate*. You learned to compare rates, to find unit rates, and to use rates to make tables and graphs and to write equations. These questions will help you summarize what you have learned:

1 Give three examples of rates.

2 How can rates or unit rates help you to make comparisons?

3 How do you convert a rate to a unit rate? Illustrate your answer with one of the examples you gave in part 1.

4 How can information about unit rates be used to make tables and graphs showing how two variables are related? Use your example to illustrate your answer.

5 How can a unit rate be used to write an equation relating two variables? Use your example to illustrate your answer.

Think about your answers to these questions, discuss your ideas with other students and your teacher, and then write a summary of your findings in your journal.

Estimating Populations and Population Densities

Since counting is one of the first mathematics skills you learned, you might expect solving a counting problem to be easy. However, sometimes counting things can get complicated.

Think about this!

How would you count the number of people attending a Fourth of July fireworks show or a human-rights rally on the mall of our nation's capital?

How would you count the number of deer in a forest, the number of fish in a stream, or the number of bees in a hive?

Share your ideas about these problems with your class. Be sure to discuss the factors that make the counting in each situation difficult.

5.1 Estimating the Size of a Crowd

News reports often give estimates of the sizes of crowds at political rallies, parades, and festivals. In 1994, television reporters announced that 350,000 people had attended a Fourth of July concert and fireworks display in front of the Capitol in Washington, D.C. How do you think this estimate was made? Do you think someone actually counted each individual in the crowd?

Problem 5.1

Sometimes the size of a crowd is estimated from aerial photographs. Imagine that the illustration below is an aerial photograph of a crowd at a rally. Each dot represents one person.

Estimate how many people attended the rally. Explain the method you used to arrive at your answer.

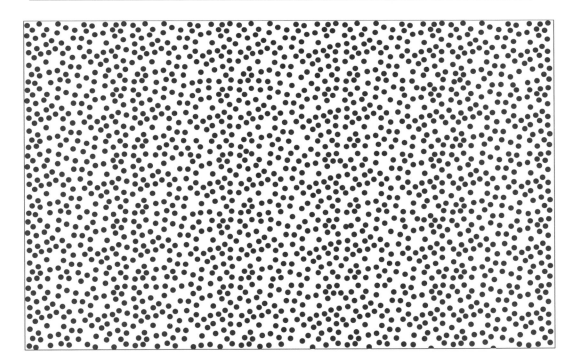

Problem 5.1 Follow-Up

In your group, discuss ways your method might lead to a poor estimate of the crowd size.

5.2 Estimating a Deer Population

In states with large populations of white-tailed deer, like Michigan, biologists in the Department of Natural Resources are asked to make estimates of deer populations. The estimates are used to set hunting seasons and regulations. But how is it possible to count all the deer in Michigan—or even in a small part of the state?

One method biologists use to count animal populations is the *capture-tag-recapture* method. You can simulate this method by using a jar or box filled with white beans. Imagine that each bean is a deer in the upper peninsula of Michigan. Your job is to estimate the number of deer without actually counting them all.

Problem 5.2

Your group will need a container with a lid and a large number of white beans. Work with your group to perform this experiment.

- Remove exactly 100 beans from the container, and mark them with a pen or marker.

- Put the marked beans back into the container, and shake or mix them with the unmarked beans.

- Without looking at the beans, scoop out a handful of about 30 beans. Record the numbers of marked and unmarked beans in this sample. Return the sample to the jar, and mix the beans together again.

- Repeat this scoop-and-count procedure four more times. In each case, record the number of marked and unmarked beans.

A. Study the data you collected. Use the data to estimate the number of beans in your container. Explain how you made your estimate.

B. Based on what you have learned from this experiment, how do you think biologists count deer populations?

■ Problem 5.2 Follow-Up

In your group, discuss ways in which this method might give a poor estimate of the actual number of deer in a population. Record your ideas.

5.3 Finding Population Densities

Sometimes a simple count does not tell you the whole story. To understand some situations, you need to count or measure two or more things and determine how the measures or counts are related. For example, suppose you are interested in how crowded a city, state, country, or other geographic region is. It is not enough to consider the number of people in the region. You must also consider the amount of available land.

Think about this!

When we reach the year 2000, there will be over 6 billion people living on our planet. But we are not evenly distributed over the 58 million square miles that make up the seven continents; some cities, states, and countries are much more crowded than others.

What do you think are the most and least crowded places on earth? How could you use land area and population data to test your ideas?

Below is a map of the United States divided into the nine regions used in reporting data from the census.

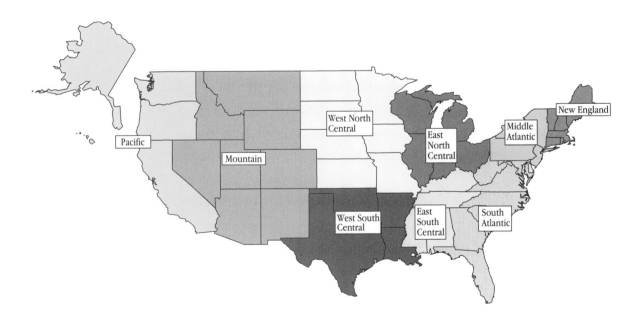

This table shows the 1994 population and land area for the nine census regions.

Region	Population	Area (square miles)
New England	13,270,000	62,811
Middle Atlantic	38,125,000	99,463
South Atlantic	46,398,000	266,221
East North Central	43,184,000	243,539
East South Central	15,890,000	178,615
West North Central	18,210,000	507,981
West South Central	28,404,000	426,234
Mountain	15,214,000	856,121
Pacific	41,645,000	895,353

Source: *Statistical Abstract of the United States 1995.* Published by the Bureau of the Census, Washington, D.C., pp. 28 and 225.

Problem 5.3

The "crowdedness" of a region is commonly reported by giving the number of people (or animals or plants) per unit of area. This rate is called the **population density** of the region.

A. What is the population density of the census region in which your school is located?

B. Divide the remaining eight census regions among the groups in your class. Find the population density of the region you are assigned. Share your group's results with the rest of the class, so that every group has data for all nine regions.

C. Order the regions from least crowded to most crowded.

D. Compare the population density of the region in which you live to the population density of each neighboring region. Write complete sentences explaining which regions you are comparing and describing how their population densities compare.

■ Problem 5.3 Follow-Up

What do you think accounts for the differences in population densities among the regions? In other words, why do you think some areas are densely populated and others are more sparsely populated?

5.4 Comparing the Dakotas

South Dakota and North Dakota rank 45 and 47 in population of all the states in the United States. South Dakota has 721,000 people in 75,896 square miles of land, and North Dakota has 638,000 people in 68,994 square miles of land.

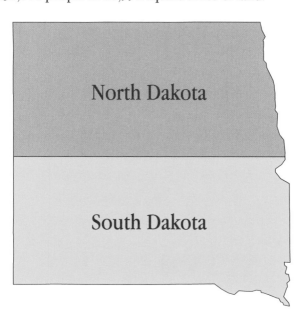

Problem 5.4

A. Which state, North Dakota or South Dakota, has the greater population density?

B. How many citizens of one state would have to move to the other state to make the population densities in the two states equal? Explain how you arrived at your answer.

■ **Problem 5.4 Follow-Up**

Find the population density of your state. How does it compare to the population densities of North and South Dakota?

5.5 Predicting Traffic Jams

You have probably been in a traffic jam or two. What kinds of things cause traffic jams? How can you predict where traffic jams are likely to occur?

One way to identify places where traffic jams are likely is by calculating traffic densities. Hong Kong is reported to have the highest traffic density in the world. In 1992, there were 418 registered cars and trucks per mile of road, or about 12.63 feet per registered vehicle! (Source: *Guinness Book of Records 1994.* Ed. Peter Matthews. New York: Bantam Books, 1994, p. 318.)

Problem 5.5

A. The city of Ole has 450,237 registered vehicles for 3000 miles of road. What is the traffic density of Ole? Calculate the number of vehicles per mile of road and the number of feet of road per vehicle.

B. The city of Driftwood Bay has 396 registered vehicles for 10 miles of road. What is the traffic density of Driftwood Bay? Calculate the number of vehicles per mile of road and the number of feet of road per vehicle.

C. Which of the three cities—Hong Kong, Ole, or Driftwood Bay—do you think is most likely to have traffic jams? Explain your answer.

D. Which of the three cities do you think is least likely to have traffic jams? Explain your answer.

■ Problem 5.5 Follow-Up

1. Other than traffic density, what factors might affect the likelihood of traffic jams?

2. A typical four-passenger car is about 13 feet long. Compare this statistic to the amount of road per mile in Hong Kong. What does this say about traffic in Hong Kong? What might Hong Kong do if this situation gets worse?

As you work on these ACE questions, use your calculator whenever you need it.

Applications

1. Yung-nan wants to estimate the number of beans in a jar. She took out a sample of 150 beans, marked them, returned them to the jar, and mixed them with the unmarked beans. She then gathered some data by taking samples. Use her data to predict the number of beans in the jar.

Sample 1
Number of marked beans: 2
Beans in sample: 25

Sample 3
Number of marked beans: 23
Beans in sample: 150

Sample 2
Number of marked beans: 10
Beans in sample: 75

Sample 4
Number of marked beans: 38
Beans in sample: 250

2. Describe a method for estimating (not counting!) the blades of grass on a football field.

3. After testing many samples, an electric company determined that approximately 2 of every 1000 light bulbs on the market are defective. Americans buy over a billion light bulbs every year. Estimate how many of these bulbs are defective.

4. Angela Krebs, a biologist, spends summers on an island off the coast of Alaska. For several summers she studied the puffin, a black-and-white seabird with a flat, brightly colored bill. Two summers ago, Angela trapped 20 puffins, then tagged and released them. This past summer, she trapped 50 puffins and found that 2 of them were tagged. She used this information to estimate the total puffin population on the island.

a. Using Angela's findings, estimate the number of puffins on the island. Explain how you made your estimate.

b. How confident are you that your estimate is accurate? Explain your answer.

In 5–8, use the data in the following table.

Population and Land Area of Selected States

State	Population	Area (square miles)
California	31,431,000	155,973
Connecticut	3,275,000	4845
New Hampshire	1,137,000	8969
North Dakota	638,000	68,994
South Dakota	721,000	75,896
Vermont	580,000	9249
Wyoming	476,000	97,105

Source: *Statistical Abstract of the United States 1995.* Published by the Bureau of the Census, Washington, D.C., pp. 28 and 225.

5. a. Find the population density of each state in the table.

b. Which state has the highest population density?

c. Which state has the lowest population density?

6. How many people would have to move from Connecticut to Wyoming to make the population densities in the two states the same? Explain.

7. How many times would the land area of Connecticut fit into the land area of Wyoming? Explain.

8. How many times greater is the population of Connecticut than the population of Wyoming? Explain.

9. The city of Canton has three parks: Flyaway Park has an area of 5000 m^2, Golden Park has an area of 7235 m^2, and Pine Park has an area of 3060 m^2.

a. At 2 P.M. last Saturday, 400 children were playing in Flyaway Park, 630 were in Golden Park, and 255 were in Pine Park. Rank the parks from least crowded to most crowded. Explain how you got your answer.

b. Oak Park is located in the suburbs of Canton. It has area of 5240 m^2. At 2 P.M. last Saturday, 462 children were playing in Oak Park. How crowded was Oak Park at this time compared to Flyaway, Golden, and Pine?

Connections

10. At Raccoon Middle School, Ms. Picadello's students conducted a class survey about their favorite rock bands. Of the 35 students in the class, 20 picked the Nerds, 8 picked the Promise, and 7 picked Willie and the Wonders.

a. If you randomly selected 10 students in the halls of Raccoon Middle School and asked what their favorite rock band was, would you expect the same ratio as in Ms. Picadello's class? Why or why not?

b. Would you expect the same ratio if you asked 10 middle-school students from another state the same question? Why or why not?

11. Shanda and Michi play a lot of basketball, and they keep a record of their free-throw attempts in practices and games. Shanda has made 500 of 1000 free-throw attempts in the last month, and Michi has made 175 of 350.

    a. Compare Shanda's and Michi's free-throw shooting.

    b. How would their success rates change if they each make their next 10 free-throw attempts? Are you surprised at the results? Why or why not?

12. The map on page 55 has a scale of about 1 inch = 600 miles. (Alaska and Hawaii are not drawn to this scale.) Excluding Alaska and Hawaii, the map is about 5 inches wide and 2.5 inches high.

    a. How could you draw a version of the map that is about 10 inches by 5 inches?

    b. What would the scale of your enlarged map be?

13. A jar contains 150 marked beans. Scott took several samples from the jar and got these results:

Beans in sample	25	50	75	100	150	200	250
Marked beans	3	12	13	17	27	38	52
Percent marked beans	12%						

    a. Copy the table, and complete the last row to show the percent of marked beans in each sample.

    b. Graph the (beans in sample, marked beans) data. Describe the pattern of data points in your graph. What does the pattern tell you about the relationship between the number of beans in a sample and the number of marked beans you can expect to find in the sample?

    c. Make a graph of the (beans in sample, percent marked beans) data. Describe the pattern of data points in your graph. What does the pattern tell you about the relationship between the number of beans in a sample and the percent of marked beans you can expect to find in the sample?

Extensions

14. Conduct an experiment in your neighborhood or school to help you predict the number of people in the United States who are left-handed. Make the assumption that your neighborhood or school is representative of the general population in left-handedness. Assume that the population of the United States is about 260 million. Describe your experiment and the results you predict for the population of the United States.

Mathematical Reflections

In this investigation, you used sampling and ratios to estimate the size of a population. You also used the idea of population density to describe and compare the "crowdedness" of geographic regions and roads. These questions will help you summarize what you have learned:

1 For each situation, explain how you could use the given information to estimate the total population of fish in the pond. Be sure to include any assumptions you make.

a. Biologists caught 25 fish in a net, tagged them, and returned them to the pond. In a later catch of 20 fish, 3 had tags.

b. Park officials tagged and released 40 fish. They kept records of the fish caught over the next month and found that 30% had tags.

2 In the problems in this investigation, what data did you need to find the densities of populations?

3 **a.** What data would you need to estimate the density of deer in a wildlife area?

b. What data would you need to estimate the density of trees in a forest?

4 Which of the following comparison statements is most like the population-density comparisons? Explain your reasoning.

a. People prefer Bolda Cola to Cola Nola by a ratio of 3 to 2.

b. Mary's car gets 30.5 miles per gallon of gas.

c. The population of California is 28,156,000 greater than the population of Connecticut.

Think about your answers to these questions, discuss your ideas with other students and your teacher, and then write a summary of your findings in your journal.

Choosing Strategies

So far in this unit, you have used fractions, percents, ratios, rates, and unit rates to make comparisons and to estimate populations and population densities. In this investigation, you will explore several problem situations in which you need to choose a strategy for solving the problem and explain why your strategy makes sense. There will usually be several ways to think about a problem. You will begin to see what kind of reasoning works best for a particular type of problem.

6.1 Scaling Up or Down

Dinosaurs (which means "terrible lizards") roamed the earth for 125 million years. By studying the bones, teeth, and footprints of these ancient reptiles, paleontologists learn more about them. Reconstructing dinosaur skeletons helps these scientists estimate the height, weight, and length of different species of dinosaur.

One of the largest predators of all time was *Tyrannosaurus rex* (which means "king tyrant lizard"). This carnivorous dinosaur lived 70 million years ago in many areas of North America, including the present states of Montana, Wyoming, and Texas. Scientists determined that *T. rex* was a meat eater by studying the shape and size of its head and teeth.

Problem 6.1

T. rex weighed about 8,100 kilograms and reached heights of up to 6 meters—almost as tall as a two-story house! Archeologists have uncovered *T. rex* skulls 1 meter long and *T. rex* incisors (the longest teeth) 15 centimeters long.

A "larger than average" human being can be about 2 meters tall and weigh 90 kilograms. Human incisors are about 1 centimeter long, and a large human skull can be about 20 centimeters long.

How big was *T. rex* compared to a "larger than average" human being?

Write a paragraph to help someone younger than you understand how the size of *T. rex* compares to the size of a human. Be very specific about the comparisons you are making.

■ Problem 6.1 Follow-Up

1. Suppose an infant *T. rex* was the same height as the human described in the problem and was similar to an adult *T. rex*. What would be the scale factor between a grown *T. rex* and the infant *T. rex*?

2. How long were the incisors of this young *T. rex*?

3. How long was the skull of this young *T. rex*?

6.2 Using Rules of Thumb

Carpenters, bakers, tailors, designers, and people in many other occupations use rules of thumb to make quick estimates. A *rule of thumb* is a method of estimating, based on experience and common sense, that is practical but not necessarily precise. For example, you may have heard someone say, "A pint is a pound the world around." This rule of thumb tells how to compare liquid measures with weight. Since 1 quart is equal to 2 pints, you can use this rule of thumb to estimate that 1 quart of milk weighs about 2 pounds. In this problem, you will be working with several rules of thumb.

Problem 6.2

In A–D, use the given rule of thumb to solve the problem. Explain how you found each answer.

A. *It takes about 100 maple trees to make 25 gallons of maple syrup.*
Mr. Paulo made maple syrup from all of his sugar maple trees. He ended up with 16 gallons of syrup. About how many sugar maple trees does he have?

B. *A 5-minute shower requires about 18 gallons of water.*
About how much water do you use for an 8-minute shower? How much water will you use if you take an 8-minute shower every day for a year?

C. *A double-spaced page of text contains about 250 words if it is printed in Times with a font size of 12, and about 330 words if it is printed in Times with a font size of 10.*
Jeremy printed his term paper in the computer lab. He used 10-point Times, and the paper came to 15 double-spaced pages. Jeremy's teacher requires term papers be 20 double-spaced pages long. If Jeremy changes the font to 12-point Times, how long will his paper be?

D. *Jogging burns about 100 calories per mile.*
Elizabeth jogs at a rate of 4.5 miles per hour. How long will it take her to burn off the 1200-calorie lunch she ate at Burger Heaven?

Adapted from *Rules of Thumb* by Tom Parker. Boston: Houghton Mifflin, 1993.

■ Problem 6.2 Follow-Up

Ask adults you know if they use any rules of thumb in their jobs or at home. Write down one of the rules you learn. Write a problem that can be solved using the rule.

Selecting Delegates

Young people all over the world are concerned about protecting and improving
the environment. American Students for the Environment is hosting a two-week
environmental studies conference for 1000 middle-school students from all over the
United States. Delegates for the conference will be selected to represent the diversity of
the United States population—geographically, ethnically, and economically. Imagine that
you are a member of the delegate selection committee.

> **American Students for the Environment**
> present
>
> **The First Annual**
>
> **ENVIRONMENTAL STUDIES CONFERENCE**
>
> *Welcome Delegates!*

Think about this!

To make fair decisions about the delegates, you must consider several
questions. Tell what information you would need to make each decision below.

- How many of the 1000 delegates should come from each of the nine census
  regions of the United States?

- What percent of the delegates should represent metropolitan areas, and
  what percent should represent rural areas?

- What percent of the delegates should represent minority groups?

You and the rest of the delegate selection committee will be using data from the 1990 United States Census to help you make your selections. To choose the number of delegates from each region, you can compare the population of each region to the population of the United States. This ratio can be written as a fraction.

$$\frac{\text{population of the region}}{\text{population of the U.S.}}$$

To give each region a fair number of delegates, it makes sense to make the ratio of delegates equivalent to the ratio of populations. This can be written as an equation:

$$\frac{\text{population of the region}}{\text{population of the U.S.}} = \frac{\text{delegates from the region}}{\text{total number of delegates}}$$

A statement about equivalent ratios or fractions, such as the one above, is called a **proportion.**

To figure out how many delegates should be chosen from a given region, you need to solve the corresponding proportion. For example, the 1990 population of the South Atlantic region of the United States was about 45 million people, and the total population of the United States was about 250 million people. To find the number of conference delegates who should come from the South Atlantic region, you need to solve the proportion

$$\frac{45,000,000}{250,000,000} = \frac{\text{delegates from South Atlantic region}}{1000}$$

Using what you know about equivalent fractions, you could write

$$\frac{45,000,000}{250,000,000} = \frac{45}{250}$$
$$= \frac{180}{1000}$$

and conclude that the South Atlantic region should have 180 delegates.

Problem 6.3

The table on pages 71 and 72 gives data about the United States population. Use the table to help you answer these questions.

A. How many of the 1000 delegates should be chosen from each of the nine geographic regions?

B. How many of the 1000 delegates should be from metropolitan areas, and how many should be from rural areas?

C. How many of the delegates should be of Hispanic origin?

D. Four racial groups are named in the data: white; black; Native American–Eskimo–Aleut; and Asian–Pacific Islander. How many of the total 1000 delegates should represent each of these races? How many should represent the category "all other races" (which is not mentioned in the data)?

E. Use your answers to A–D to help you develop a plan for selecting the delegates. Describe your plan in a report that you could submit to the conference organizers.

■ Problem 6.3 Follow-Up

If you could add another criterion to help choose the delegates so that the representation would be fair, what criterion would you add and why?

U.S. 1990 Population by Region, Race, and Metro/Rural Location
(All Numbers in 1000s)

	Total	Metro areas	Rural areas	White	Black	Hispanic*	Native American, Eskimo, Aleut	Asian, Pacific Islander
United States	**248,710**	**192,726**	**55,984**	**199,686**	**29,986**	**22,354**	**1959**	**7274**
New England	**13,207**	**10,598**	**2609**	**12,033**	**628**	**568**	**33**	**232**
Maine	1228	441	787	1208	5	7	6	7
New Hampshire	1109	622	487	1087	7	11	2	9
Vermont	563	131	431	555	2	4	2	3
Massachusetts	6016	5438	578	5405	300	288	12	143
Rhode Island	1003	928	75	917	39	46	4	18
Connecticut	3287	3038	250	2859	274	213	7	51
Middle Atlantic	**37,602**	**34,193**	**3409**	**30,036**	**4986**	**3186**	**92**	**1104**
New York	17,990	16,386	1605	13,385	2859	2214	63	694
New Jersey	7730	7730	n/a	6130	1037	740	15	273
Pennsylvania	11,882	10,077	1805	10,520	1090	232	15	137
East North Central	**42,009**	**32,557**	**9452**	**35,764**	**4817**	**1438**	**150**	**573**
Ohio	10,847	8567	2280	9522	1155	140	20	91
Indiana	5544	3796	1748	5021	432	99	13	38
Illinois	11,431	9450	1981	8953	1694	904	22	285
Michigan	9295	7446	1850	7756	1292	202	56	105
Wisconsin	4892	3298	1593	4513	245	93	39	54
West North Central	**17,660**	**10,132**	**7528**	**16,254**	**899**	**289**	**188**	**195**
Minnesota	4375	2960	1415	4130	95	54	50	78
Iowa	2777	1223	1554	2683	48	33	7	25
Missouri	5117	3387	1730	4486	548	62	20	41
North Dakota	639	257	381	604	4	5	26	3
South Dakota	696	205	491	638	3	5	51	3
Nebraska	1578	766	812	1481	57	37	12	12
Kansas	2478	1333	1145	2232	143	94	22	32
South Atlantic	**43,567**	**32,461**	**11,106**	**33,391**	**8924**	**2133**	**172**	**631**
Delaware	666	442	224	535	112	16	2	9
Maryland	4781	4439	343	3394	1190	125	13	140
District of Columbia	607	607	n/a	180	400	33	1	11
Virginia	6187	4483	1704	4792	1163	160	15	159
West Virginia	1793	653	1140	1726	56	8	2	7
North Carolina	6629	3758	2871	5008	1456	77	80	52
South Carolina	3487	2113	1374	2407	1040	31	8	22
Georgia	6478	4212	2266	4600	1747	109	13	76
Florida	12,938	11,754	1184	10,749	1760	1574	36	154
East South Central	**15,176**	**8513**	**6663**	**12,049**	**2977**	**95**	**41**	**84**
Kentucky	3685	1714	1971	3392	263	22	6	18
Tennessee	4877	3300	1577	4048	778	33	10	32
Alabama	4041	2723	1317	2976	1021	25	17	22
Mississippi	2576	776	1798	1633	915	16	9	13

	Total	Metro areas	Rural areas	White	Black	Hispanic*	Native American, Eskimo, Aleut	Asian, Pacific Islander
West South Central	**26,703**	**19,614**	**7,089**	**20,142**	**3929**	**4539**	**350**	**407**
Arkansas	2351	943	1408	1945	374	20	13	13
Louisiana	4220	2935	1285	2839	1299	93	19	41
Oklahoma	3146	1870	1276	2584	234	86	252	34
Texas	16,987	13,867	3119	12,775	2022	4340	66	319
Mountain	**13,659**	**9179**	**4480**	**11,762**	**374**	**1992**	**481**	**217**
Montana	799	191	608	741	2	12	48	4
Idaho	1007	206	801	950	3	53	14	9
Wyoming	454	134	319	427	4	26	9	3
Colorado	3294	2686	608	2905	133	424	28	60
New Mexico	1515	733	782	1146	30	579	134	14
Arizona	3665	2896	769	2963	111	688	204	55
Utah	1723	1336	387	1616	12	85	24	33
Nevada	1202	996	206	1013	79	124	20	38
Pacific	**39,127**	**35,479**	**3648**	**28,255**	**2454**	**8114**	**453**	**3831**
Washington	4867	3976	891	4309	150	215	81	211
Oregon	2842	1947	895	2637	46	113	38	69
California	29,760	28,493	1267	20,524	2209	7688	242	2846
Alaska	550	226	324	415	22	18	86	20
Hawaii	1108	836	272	370	27	81	5	685

*Persons of Hispanic origin may be of any race.

Totals include other races, which are not shown separately. N/A means not applicable.

Source: *Statistical Abstract of the United States 1993.* Published by the Bureau of the Census, Washington, D.C., p. 254.

As you work on these ACE questions, use your calculator whenever you need it.

Applications

1. In a free-throw contest at the environmental studies conference, Clifford, a delegate from New England, made 10 out of 15 shots. Suppose Clifford's success rate stays the same for his next 100 shots. Write and solve proportions to answer these questions.

   a. How many shots will Clifford make out of his next 60 shots?

   b. How many shots will Clifford make out of his next 80 shots?

   c. How many shots will it take for Clifford to make 30 more free-throws?

   d. How many shots will it take for him to make 45 more free-throws?

2. The conference organizers ordered environmental buttons for the participants to wear. They paid $18 for 12 dozen buttons. Write and solve proportions to answer these questions.

   a. How much do 4 dozen buttons cost?

   b. How much do 50 dozen buttons cost?

   c. How many dozens of buttons can the organizers buy for $27?

   d. How many dozens of buttons can the organizers buy for $63?

3. Middletown decided to sponsor a two-day meeting for its own middle-school students to study local environmental problems. There are three middle schools in Middletown: Red Middle School with 618 students, White Middle School with 378 students, and Blue Middle School with 204 students. If 20 student delegates in all will attend the conference, how many should be selected from each school?

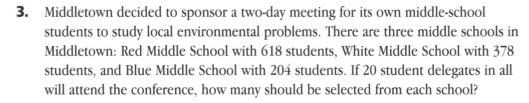

4. This table gives the total land area of each census region in the United States.

Census region	Area (square miles)
New England	62,811
Middle Atlantic	99,463
East North Central	266,221
West North Central	243,539
South Atlantic	178,615
East South Central	507,981
West South Central	426,234
Mountain	856,121
Pacific	895,353

a. Suppose the delegates for the environmental conference in Problem 6.3 were selected using the ratio of the area of the census region to the area of the United States. Use the data above to figure out how many delegates should attend from each region.

b. In part a, you determined the number of delegates from each region by comparing land areas. In part A of Problem 6.3, you determined the number of delegates from each region by comparing populations. For each region, discuss how these numbers compare.

c. Give one reason why each system of choosing delegates (using land areas or using populations) might be fair.

5. Swimming a quarter of a mile burns about the same number of calories as running a mile.

a. Gilda runs a 26-mile marathon. How far would her sister have to swim to burn the same number of calories Gilda burned during the marathon?

b. Jack swims 5 miles a day. How many miles would he have to run to burn the same number of calories he burns during his daily swim?

Connections

6. Which is the better buy: a 14-ounce box of Cruncho cereal for $1.98, or a 36-ounce box of Cruncho cereal for $2.59?

7. Which is the better average: 10 free-throws out of 15, or 8 free-throws out of 10?

8. Which is the better home-run rate: hitting 2 home runs in 6 times at bat, or hitting 5 home runs in 12 times at bat?

9. The population of the United States in 1994 was about 260,651,000. The land area of the United States is 3,536,338 square miles. If the people in the United States were spread uniformly throughout the states, how many people would there be per square mile? Compare your answer with the population density of your state.

10. The picture below is drawn on a centimeter grid.

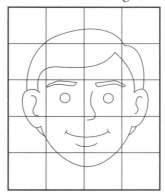

a. On a grid made of larger squares than those shown here, draw a figure similar to this figure. What is the scale factor between the original figure and your drawing?

b. Draw another figure similar to this one, but use a grid made of smaller squares than those shown here. What is the scale factor between the original and your drawing?

11. Anna is making a circular spinner to be used at the school carnival. She wants the spinner to be divided so that 30% of the area is blue, 20% is red, 15% is green, and 35% is yellow. Design a spinner that meets her specifications.

Extensions

12. Below is a table of data from a middle school class showing each student's household's water use for one week and the number of people in the household.

Our Water Use

Student (initials)	People in household	Water use (gallons)	Rate of water use (gallons/person)
RE	5	1901	
TW	4	1682	
HW	5	1493	
WE	4	1336	
GK	5	1332	
DJ	6	1309	
MJ	5	1231	
WD	5	1231	
MA	5	1204	
LR	5	1031	
FP	4	986	
HA	5	985	
TB	3	940	
CH	5	938	
ME	4	924	
JW	4	910	
PR	4	843	
NP	3	819	
BH	4	807	
EB	4	755	
PJ	4	726	
HJ	4	641	
HM	3	554	
JZ	2	493	

a. Calculate the rate of water use per person in each household.

b. Combine all the data to find the rate of water use overall.

c. Round your answers in part a to the nearest 10. Make a stem plot showing the rate of water use per person in each household. Start your stem plot like this:

```
4 | 2
3 | 8 0
2 |
1 |
```

Key

4 | 2 means 420

d. The two *histograms* below and on the next page display the information about gallons of water used per person in each household. Compare the two histograms and explain how they differ.

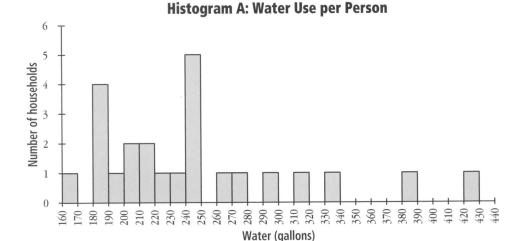

Histogram A: Water Use per Person

Histogram B: Water Use per Person

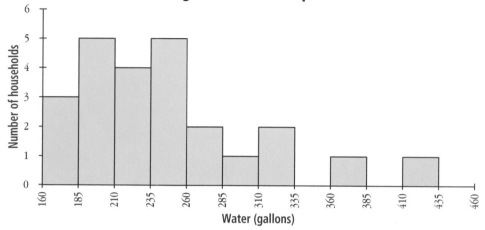

e. Does your stem plot from part c look like either histogram?

f. Suppose a new student joined the class and her household used 270 gallons of water per person. How would this student's data be indicated on Histogram A and Histogram B?

g. What is the typical number of gallons of water used per person in one week? Justify your answer, using Histograms A and B and your stem plot to help you explain.

h. Make Histogram C by grouping the data in intervals of 30 gallons. Now which graph—A, B, or C—would be the most useful to help you answer the question in part g? Why?

13. The people of the United States are represented in Congress in two ways: each state has representatives in the House of Representatives, and each state has senators in the Senate.

a. The number of representatives from each state in the House of Representatives varies from state to state. How is the number of representatives from each state determined?

b. How is the number of senators from each state determined?

c. Compare the two methods of determining representation in Congress. What are the advantages and disadvantages of these two forms of representation?

A meeting of the House of Representatives

14. The very small country of Trig has three states: Sine, Cosine, and Tangent, with populations of 59, 76, and 14, respectively. The Trig Congress has 35 members.

    a. Using a method that you think is fair to all states, determine the number of representatives from each state. Explain your reasoning.

    b. How would the number of representatives from each state change if there were 37 members of Congress?

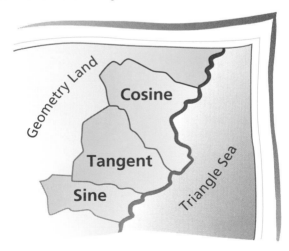

15. Ryan asked his family to mark on a chart whenever they washed a load of laundry. Here is his family's chart for one week:

	Sun.	Mon.	Tues.	Wed.	Thurs.	Fri.	Sat.
Large load					X		
Medium load		X		X	X		
Small load			X		X		

a. Using the following information about rate of water use, estimate the total amount of water Ryan's family used for washing laundry during the week. Explain your answer.

Large-capacity washing machines use approximately
- 9.5 gallons of water for a small load
- 13.4 gallons of water for a medium load
- 17.3 gallons of water for a large load

b. If this is a typical week, how much water does Ryan's family use in one year for washing laundry?

Mathematical Reflections

In this investigation, you used ratios, rates, percents, fractions, and proportions to solve problems. You thought about which methods of making comparisons would be helpful in solving particular types of problems. These questions will help you summarize what you have learned:

1 **a.** Describe a situation in which finding a rate is a good strategy for making comparisons. Tell why you think your situation calls for finding a rate.

b. Describe a situation in which finding a unit rate is a good strategy for making comparisons. Tell why you think your situation calls for finding a unit rate.

2 There are 17 girls and 13 boys in Mr. Baldridge's class. Write every comparison you can think of that can be formed from this information. Describe what each comparison shows.

3 Rodrigo drove his car 400 miles and used 12 gallons of gas. Write two rates that tell about this situation, and explain what each shows.

4 If you know that 4 cans of chili feed 6 people, how many cans of chili will feed 240 people? How many people can you feed with 45 cans of chili? Explain your answers.

5 How do you recognize a situation in which you need to use a ratio comparison rather than simply finding differences?

Think about your answers to these questions, discuss your ideas with other students and your teacher, and then write a summary of your findings in your journal.

Paper Pool

The project is a mathematical investigation of a new game called Paper Pool. For a pool table, use grid paper rectangles like the one shown at right. Each corner is a pocket where a ball could stop.

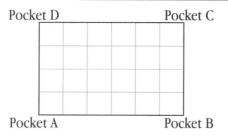

How To Play Paper Pool

- The ball always starts at corner A.
- To start the imaginary ball rolling, hit it with an imaginary cue stick.
- The ball always moves on a 45° diagonal across the grid.
- When the ball hits a side of the table it bounces off at a 45° angle and continues its travel.
- If the ball hits a corner pocket, it falls in and stops.

The dotted lines on the table at the right show the ball's path.

- The ball stopped at corner D.
- It got 5 hits (including the starting hit and the final hit).
- The dimensions of the table are 6 by 4 (always mention the horizontal length first).

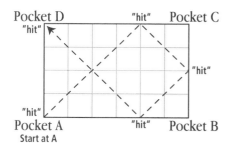

Part 1: Investigate Two Questions

Use Paper Pool Labsheets U.P.A, U.P.B, and U.P.C to play the game. Try to find a rule that tells you (1) the corner where the ball will stop and (2) the number of hits it will make along the way. Keep track of the dimensions because they may give you clues to a pattern.

Part 2: Write a Report

When you find some patterns and reach some conclusions, write a report that includes:

1. A list of the rules you found and why you think they are correct.

2. Drawings of grid paper tables that show your rule.

3. Any tables, charts, or other tools that helped you find patterns.

4. Other patterns or ideas about Paper Pool.

Extension Question

Can you predict the length of the ball's path on any size Paper Pool table? Each time the ball crosses a square, the length is 1 diagonal unit. Find the length of the ball's path in diagonal units for any dimension.

Glossary

population density The population density is the average number of things (people, animals, and so on) per unit of area (or, less commonly, the average amount of space per person or animal). Population density indicates how crowded a region is and can be calculated as the ratio of population to area.

proportion An equation stating that two ratios are equal. For example:

$$\frac{\text{hours spent on homework}}{\text{hours spent in school}} = \frac{2}{7}$$

Note that this does not necessarily imply that "hours spent on homework" = 2 or that "hours spent in school" = 7. During a week, 10 hours may have been spent on homework while 35 hours were spent in school. The proportion is still true because $\frac{10}{35} = \frac{2}{7}$.

rate A comparison of the quantities of two different units or objects is called a rate. A rate can be thought of as a direct comparison of two sets (20 cookies for 5 children) or as an average amount (4 cookies per child). A rate such as 5.5 miles per hour can be written as $\frac{5.5 \text{ miles}}{1 \text{ hour}}$, or 5.5 miles : 1 hour.

ratio A ratio is a comparison of two quantities that tells the scale between them. Ratios may be expressed as quotients, fractions, decimals, percents, or given in the form a:b. Here are some examples of uses of ratios:

- The ratio of females to males on the swim team is 2 to 3, or $\frac{2 \text{ females}}{3 \text{ males}}$.
- The train travels at a speed of 80 miles per hour, or $\frac{80 \text{ miles}}{1 \text{ hour}}$.
- If a small figure is enlarged by a scale factor of 2, the new figure will have an area four times its original size. The ratio of the small figure's area to the large figure's area will be $\frac{1}{4}$. The ratio of the large figure's area to the small figure's area will be $\frac{4}{1}$ or 4.

- In the example above, the ratio of the length of a side of the small figure to the length of the corresponding side of the large figure is $\frac{1}{2}$. The ratio of the length of a side in the large figure to the length of the corresponding side in the small figure is $\frac{2}{1}$, or 2.

scale, scaling The scale is the number a ratio is multiplied by to find an equivalent ratio. Scaling a ratio produces any number of equivalent ratios, which all have the same units. For example, multiplying the rate of 4.5 gallons per hour by a scale of 2 yields the rate of 9 gallons per 2 hours. Scales are also used on maps to give the relationship between a measurement on the map to the actual physical measurement.

unit rate A unit rate compares an amount to a single unit. For example, 1.9 children per family, 32 mpg, and $\frac{3 \text{ flavors of ice cream}}{1 \text{ banana split}}$ are unit rates. Unit rates are often found by scaling other rates.

Index